WHY GORE WILL WIN IN 2000

WHY GORE WILL WIN IN 2000

▼

Steven A. Ludsin

Writers Club Press

San Jose New York Lincoln Shanghai

Why Gore Will Win in 2000

Writers Club Press
an imprint of iUniverse.com, Inc.

For information address:
iUniverse.com, Inc.
620 North 48th Street, Suite 201
Lincoln, NE 68504-3467
www.iuniverse.com

ISBN: 0-595-12733-9

Printed in the United States of America

CONTENTS

DECEMBER 1, 1998

▼

It is poetic that we begin this prediction that Gore and the Democrats will prevail in the 2000 elections. It is a simple status quo analysis. The current economy is strong and the pundits have been missing the target. Matt Winkler, Editor in Chief of Bloomberg News and I had lunch to celebrate Chuck Schumer's election victory. I was propounding my various political theories to Matt and at the end of our luncheon I agreed to write a book that will predict the outcome of the national elections in the year 2000. It is important to note that this was written with foresight and edited in hindsight. I will contrast conventional wisdom (cw) with the probabilistic scenario (ps). Being a contrarian, the probable scenario represents the best prediction by looking behind the developments to decide the outcome.

A few buzz phrases come to mind, but one that gnaws at me is the concept of a parallel universe. The pundits in DC are living in a world that is detached in too many ways from the everyday lives of Middle America. The dinner parties and the secretiveness that accompanies that world are confined to the elite. Consequently their intake is narrow and limited to people who confirm the view that is held collectively but in isolation. The Presidential election is like a rugby game with both teams hovering over the ball fighting for something I have never understood in rugby but in the election it's the center.

Vice President Gore wins because it's his to lose. He is in the incumbent position and the charm of Clinton has rubbed off on Gore. Conversely, Gore doesn't have the baggage of Bill Clinton, but President Clinton had to be the flawed talent he is in order to have penetrated the Republican hold on the White House. We now have the battle of the baby boomers. George W. Bush Jr. and compassionate conservatism won't cut it. He is a potent candidate, but a son in his father's business is always compared to dad and is fighting a private battle that will negatively affect his resolve.

As for Congress, the parallel universe of the House members aping the Lions, Rotary and Masons of their districts keeps a similar narrowness of the dinner party set, but is a result of the constant fundraising from the interests that are also a limited slice of life of America. Make no mistake about it; it is all about money. He who has the war chest wins or at least has a fighting chance to participate.

The Clinton opponents always overplay their hand and the Republicans will continue that self-destructive behavior. Chuck Schumer was willing to stand toe to toe with Al D'Amato the ultimate unabashed caricature of the political animal saying what he needs to with little regard to principle. It caught up with D'Amato and it will catch up with the Republicans. Henry Hyde is trying to stretch his mandate in the impeachment proceedings to the fund raising of the Clinton Reelection in 1996. The Senate Committee and the House Committee that already investigated could not make anything stick, so Hyde and the headhunters of his committee want to recycle the investigations. This is a desperate effort to push President Clinton out of office for something that doesn't constitute an impeachable event. Nevertheless, the Republicans won't give up and that overreaching will be their own undoing.

Status Quo

If President Clinton ran against himself he would have lost in 1996, but god blessed him with Bob Dole. Similarly Vice President Gore will have providence shine upon him and it is his to lose. Status quo has its own rewards and the distraction of the impeachment proceedings will reveal the Republicans as a party avoiding analysis of troubling social issues and only holding on to hot button issues to keep the focus so narrow as to cut them from the electorate. In foreign affairs there was a movement that was so narrow it was deemed a form of idiocy. The Republicans are now practicing this approach in domestic affairs. It will hand the majority back to the Democrats.

The poetry of starting this prediction on December 1, 1998 is that it's the fifth anniversary of the day Erskine B. Bowles gave me a yes for my pilot program for selling assets of the SBA on the Bloomberg. That experience made this book possible. I have the caricature that sadly is embodied in a real human being, Arnold S. Rosenthal. He is fat and unhappy. A numbers cruncher turned policy person. I had the misfortune of having a contract that was implemented by Rosenthal and his department. I will spare you the gory details, but Rosenthal is a useful frame of reference. After the Republican policies become law, it is our unfortunate fate to have the Arnies of the world implement those policies. This is a dangerous combination of ignorance and arrogance. The increased exposure of the DC world thanks to the information dissemination increased through Internet and computer technology will result in the extinction of the under qualified staff person of the federal agencies. More people will have the courage to confront these limited people from arbitrarily making it up as they go along.

There will be a flight to quality to candidates that have something to offer. Ironically the overwhelming cost of getting elected will bring a higher quality product in the form of a well honed, well-informed individual capable of being nimble enough to react to the constant changes our fast paced world requires.

Bob Torricelli became the head of the Senate Campaign Committee. He is a baby boomer who rose to power quickly. The comment about the positive attitude of the Democrats is the switch from the defensive to the offensive. The Republicans kept all their leadership in place. In politics, follow the money: Senator McConnell held on to his leadership of the Republican Senatorial Campaign Committee. The status quo prevails.

Vice President Gore addressed his natural base, the Democratic Leadership Council. The potential candidates are declaring themselves: Bradley, Kerrey, Kerry and Wellstone. I believe the winner after Gore becomes the vice presidential candidate. A beauty contest needs a runner up and that person could be vice president. The Gore campaign will be aided by the cannibalism of the Republicans. Their extremism will make the chance for the White House diminished. Congressional Republicans are still reeling from Gingrich's resignation. Michael Forbes of Long Island goes from outcast to inner circle to Robert Livingston and that ascent is too sudden too last. The darker forces of the Republican Party will keep the party divided. Democrats can raise money with business due to the stronger economy and still use the grass roots voter turnout of the unions and the black community.

IMPEACHMENT

▼

The Republicans intend to quicken the pace of the impeachment proceedings. It is hard to believe they think the alleged perjury, which must be committed knowingly and on a material issue, is an impeachable offense. The obsession with Clinton's demise will further isolate the Republican Party.

I had a chance to speak with Mayor Guiliani's assistant, Dennison Young. The Mayor has become a national figure, and the improved perception of New York City is palpable. Whether that translates to a viable place on a national ticket remains to be seen. The center is the source of presidential success, but there is a concern that the extreme right will not give ground in order to nominate a centrist candidate.

There is a little excitement percolating about the potential challengers to Vice President Gore and Governor Bush. The need for funds is so insatiable that few candidates can mount a realistic challenge.

The chance for campaign reform is slim. After all, incumbents enjoy the advantage and it is so vital to political survival that they are unlikely to give it up.

The End of the Clinton Presidency

I feel a sense of loss about the closing days of the Clinton Presidency. I remember the thrill of the signed letters in cardboard from the White House. I may have been naïve, but my ideas were getting through. I can't help but think that previous respect for my opinion will evaporate because I had the misfortune of dealing with intractable individuals at the SBA. Perhaps it was my rite of passage, I earned my stripes and even though it isn't the equivalent of military service, I did a form of public service.

There is a common notion that dealing with the government is at one's own peril. That makes me very uncomfortable. Nevertheless, politics is in my veins and I'm not a crusader, but I can't abandon the process. So raising funds and support for a candidate that may understand the need for intelligent governance is worthwhile. I may be working against a candidate as much as I may be working for his opponent. Sadly, the voters are confronting the choice of a candidate they may not be enthusiastic about, but they also have the opportunity to vote against the candidate that is further from their agenda. The question remains what is the agenda when the economy is strong and there is relative peace internationally?

Republicans drop the campaign finance inquiry as part of the impeachment process. This is a retreat and the Republicans are painting themselves into a corner. The Congress is suffering from the same insularity as the pundits. The Democrats can be cautious and address the electorate's concerns such as Social Security, education, the economy, etc. Vice President Gore addressed the Democratic Leadership Council and used the phrase pragmatic idealism as a counterpoint to compassionate conservatism. I'm not sure the theme is captivating but it is a useful comparison.

Senator Bradley announced his presidential quest. I was taken aback by the observation of the Quinipiac College pollster that Bradley would deal with the race relations issue, because of his basketball experience. It seemed superficial and I raise the question as to whether America is willing or interested in dealing with race relations. Senator Bradley could be formidable, but I believe he becomes number 2.

I believe President Clinton has weathered the storm again and the Republican right is running out of steam and will have to face the remaining Clinton Presidency. I can help but feel that my prophecy could be self-fulfilling, but the obsession with hot button social issues will backfire. Democracy has some hope, but I think there is still a backdoor to the process, campaign contributions. It is a rich man's game.

The juxtaposition of the unemployment numbers of 4.4% and the picture of Bill Bradley captured the dilemma of the Gore challengers. How do you distinguish yourself from a Vice President who has overseen the economic recovery and is associated with a popular president? It is Gore's to lose, but a lucky challenger could be the lead dog if some negatives hit Gore. Otherwise it will be a refinement of issues that will ultimately separate the Democrats from the Republicans. Practical idealism is a start but certainly not the last word.

President Clinton's lawyers properly requested the House Judiciary committee to allow the White House attorneys to defend the President. The importance of an impeachment cannot be overstated. The procedure sounds like a legal proceeding, but the political considerations override concerns for legal formalities. Therefore it is wise to invoke all efforts to protect the President and maintain due process. It sounds like a civics lesson, but the vehemence of the Republican Right requires a balanced process. After 40 years in the minority in Congress it's like the poltergeist screaming from the grave. Checks and balances underpin the system and the tension in the coming weeks underscore the similarity of the partisan process in Congress with litigation: controlled hostility and constant jousting. Litigators relish the process and the American people are now getting a bird's eye view of the cold-blooded process called litigation.

The impeachment of the President movement gains momentum, and yet it ignores the Republican's abiding fear, Vice President Gore becomes a sitting President. Be careful about what you want, you might get it. The President practices business as usual and it seems to keep the opposition off balance. The roster of Democratic hopefuls is attractive. The Republicans are losing appeal by remaining too bent on the removal of the President for offenses which are not impeachable offenses. Coups are more common in South America, Africa or other areas with less secure governments.

The economy moves forward with wishes for a 10,000 Dow index. I saw Bush's response to Gore criticism of the compassionate conservatism as an example of Bush oratorical flourish, with Bush characterizing Gore's comments as "odd"; an example of classic Bush "Softspeak" to the maximum of neutral. The fight for the center may well be the consistent approach of being non-controversial almost to the point of boredom. I think there has to be some battle lines drawn and a continued effort to find issues that move the voters without being hot button social issues that divide the voters and increase negative campaigning. Certainly pocketbook issues will fit that agenda. Throw in education, medical care, stable inflation and growth and the stew will sell. Issues matter but so does character.

Vice President Gore's father died at the age of 90. He lost reelection to Bill Brock, who coincidentally replaced me on the U.S. Holocaust Memorial Council. Gore Senior lost because of his early opposition to the Vietnam War. It occurred to me that the apple doesn't roll far from the tree and that I always believed there was a strain of character in the Gore family. It gives some historical perspective to the potential race between Gore, the son of a Senator and Bush, the son of a Congressman who became Vice President and President.

Baby Boomers

I plan to have cocktails with Bill Heyman an old friend. In some ways our friendship is a microcosm of the baby boomer political evolution. Bill has raised money for Republicans, particularly President Bush. He was awarded a senior position at the SEC. Now he intends to return to the Bush cause. He has been successful on Wall Street and I expect he could do well in the jockeying for position in the Bush election team in New York.

I haven't raised the kind of money Bill has been able to raise and unfortunately I don't have the personal funds since you need long legs to run with the big dogs in the tall grass as LBJ used to say. I believed Bill was picking my brain to reflect opposition thinking to the Bush campaign when Dukakis was the nominee. I'm not sure my input changed the outcome, but it is interesting to keep your finger on the pulse of the opposition.

The impeachment defense helped the President. The Republicans have lost a sense of proportion. The facts don't warrant impeachment. How this impacts the presidential race remains to be seen, but I think the overreaching of President Clinton's opponents will accrue to Vice President Gore's benefit.

The narrowness of the Republicans will haunt them. There is a dangerous self-righteousness, which will undercut the Republican Party's goals whatever they may be. Senator Ashcroft got it right when he said that the Republicans are being defined by what divides them. Those divisions will become more pronounced in the primary season and the Democrats can benefit by addressing the voter's concerns and responding to the morality charges as they develop, but remaining on the offense on the issues.

The holiday season allows for some peace. House Republican Judiciary Committee members avoided the annual White House Holiday festivities. The stubbornness will be their undoing, but impeachment was taken very seriously. Gore is taking advantage of incumbency by convening a conference on global efforts to fight corruption and safeguard integrity among justice and security officials. The moderates will determine the outcome of the impeachment vote and the congressional leadership does not get the fact that it is the moderates that will get them into the White House. The Op Ed piece on Michael Huffington who spent 30 million of his personal fortune shows the disturbing influence of cold cash on the political process and while he was at it, he also came out of the closet.

Rep. Amos Houghton will not vote for impeachment and in his Op Ed piece. He stated it has often been said that when the only tool you own is a hammer sooner or later everything begins to look like a nail. We should search for other tools in our tool chest. I am reminded of a companion theory if charm fails use the hammer. The Republicans assume charm fails without trying. Meanwhile, Vice president Gore buries his father and that symbolizes the transition of power to the baby boomers.

The president is flying to the Middle East while the House is prosecuting articles of impeachment. The Republicans are ignoring the hole theory and are digging themselves deeper everyday. The Republican presidential primary players are keeping a low profile. Gore would be the incumbent president if impeachment occurs. The hypocrisy of the Republicans is the convenient amnesia as to previous instances of presidential misstatements.

President Clinton expressed his shame. I believe the obsession and overreaching by the-Republicans will lead to the president's renewal. The outcome is preordained. The Senate will not remove him from office. The Democrats can set the legislative agenda while the Republicans remain distracted.

The campaign handicapping continues. President Clinton won't resign. The Republicans would like a bloodless coup. The rest of the field of Democrats is starting to create buzz. The economy stays strong, mergers continue and America is the pre-eminent power. Politics is an overnight business. The groundwork is laid and the outcome of the Clinton Presidency is already a tarnished legacy but one of achievement.

Senator Kerrey has decided not to run for President. I thought he would be a strong contender and this confirmed Gore's inside position in the horserace.

The nation's Republican governors are far from enthusiastic supporters of the impeachment process against President Clinton, which most of them see as distracting Congress from more important business.

"I'm sick and tired of this," Louisiana Gov. Mike Foster said in a weekend statement. "I think the whole country is sick and tired of this, and if they don't get this over with, and get it off the front page, there's going to be hell to pay."

The Republicans will self-destruct in this impeachment process. The impeachment fever rises and the campaign is quietly going about its business. The President is acting Presidential and carrying out the peacemaker role in Israel. The split Presidency is a model for the relentlessness required for a presidential race. Ignore the negatives and play up the positives. Compartmentalization is key to surviving the Presidential race. It appears the field will be narrow and the demands on the candidates are enormous. I believe Gore has more fire in hi belly than observers would notice. It is almost a distraction to the campaign that pundits are focusing on a lame duck President and his alleged impeachable offenses. The time to fix the roof is when the sun shines in. Keep at it Democrats because you have now distracted the opposition and they will be blindsided by their own monomaniacal pursuit of a President who they envy and who is leaving anyhow.

Cw: High-mindedness appeals to the electorate. Ps: Perception of hard work and constituent service is more satisfying to the voters.

Erskine B. Bowles decided not to run for Governor of North Carolina. Perhaps Vice President Gore has persuaded him to stay loose for 2000. Gore decided to remain in DC for the historic impeachment vote in the House on Thursday. The folks I speak with are disappointed with the Republicans for being so dogged in their pursuit. The public's view of the process may further erode voter turnout and that has pro incumbent consequences. The fact is that the second Clinton term has been about keeping Gore as the successor and the impeachment will harm Clinton's legacy but probably not hurt Vice President Gore.

We are in store for some drama, near term, but the outcome is now becoming clearer. The Congress is in a parallel universe with its own party. What is it that possesses the Republican Right to be so uncompromising and go down in flames?

A knowledgeable friend said it all when we were watching CNN broadcasting a town meeting held by Congressman Chris Shays about impeachment. His line was change the channel, forget impeachment, we just invaded Iraq. The President escalated the battle by finally launching the attack due to Iraq's defiance of the weapons inspectors from the United Nations. There appears to be impatience with both parties at the impeachment process, but the President certainly stalled the momentum. The Republicans are going to vote the impeachment on Friday the 18th, but the election will be impacted for years to come. Perhaps this is a seismic shift in the political process where the rules become less important and the battle becomes a zero sum game. All pretense at bi-partisanship seems swept away. The chance for change remains slim because only a minority of America votes and the outcome is determined by the activists, not the disaffected.

I believe the Republicans are listening to the echoes of their own voices and narrowing their field of hearing. Perhaps Congressman Shays' town meeting is a harbinger of the moderate Republicans effort to listen to the electorate.

Rep. Livingston, the Speaker of the House after Newt Gingrich, revealed an extra marital affair, which undercuts the moral high ground taken by the Republicans. The impeachment will be voted and the Iraq invasion continues. Now everyone is compartmentalizing. The irony is that everyone copies President Clinton and then scorns him. Fortunately Vice President Gore is fighting mad and the hunting season is opening early with or without permits.

Ironically now that the hunting season is open, I believe there are more active participants than usual. The telephone lines to Congress were flooded. The trial of the President should inflame passions even more. As Einstein said, from clutter create simplicity, from discord create harmony and in difficulty lies opportunity.

The Democrats are still having difficulty getting used to being the minority in the House and to a lesser degree in the Senate. At this point it appears there is less pretense about bi-partisanship. As they said in All the President's Men, follow the money. Today leadership is based on fundraising capability.

The President spoke in the Rose Garden on the Saturday after the articles of impeachment was voted by the House. The preface was a walk by the

President, Hillary, Vice President Gore, Dick Gephardt and John Podesta. The show of support is strong. The Republicans have taken the gloves off and the atmosphere is poisoned. This episode created an opportunity to seize the middle and assure Democratic victories in 2000.

Vendetta

James Carville said it well when he said the vendetta would be at the polls. People will be bringing box lunches. The irony is that this ordeal of venomous discourse that somehow isn't "personal" is hard to accept. So the race is on. President Clinton knew after his reelection that the name of the game was keeping the White Hose for the Democrats. It is similar to a father passing on the reins to the next generation and realizing the moral compromises that it took to get there while believing the next generation won't have to compromise itself as much.

The visibility of Gore and Gephardt portends the creation of a team for 2000. The question remains as to how to unseat the Republican incumbents in the House. The issues are education, social security, Medicare, and as always the economy.

Dennis Hastert becomes Speaker because of what he is not, instead of because of what he is.

That is a tacit concession that business as usual for the Republican leadership is over. The right wing of the party is calling the shots. The polarization is evident when you see Geraldo Rivera and Gordon Liddy duking it out on the NBC morning talk show. Forget the fact that Geraldo is an interviewer on his own NBC show; it indicates the emotionalism and sensationalism of television journalism, which reflects magazine journalism and newspaper journalism in one seamless presentation; it has found a home in the impeachment story. Washington has eclipsed Hollywood for scandals and alleged corruption. The Hollywood sneak and pry journalism portrayed by Danny DeVito's character in L.A. Confidential is honing in on Washington. Larry Flynt has sensationalized politics by exposing something everyone took for granted but was willing to ignore, electoral infidelity. It was like alcoholism, acknowledged but ignored until it went too far and damaged more than the drinker.

Shift in the House

The moderates who voted for impeachment now reveal they don't want removal, only censure. This illustrates the difficulty of voting for legislation that you don't embrace but are afraid that future opponents will distort. This brings me to the observation that sets up the change in the House in 2000. The Democrats are going on the offense to challenge the shaky districts and the Republicans who voted for impeachment. I guess the opportunity became obvious, but the activism that may result might breathe life into an indifferent electorate.

The Holiday season creates a short respite from the saturation media coverage of the impeachment. Vice President Gore seems to have a no lose situation. He appears loyal and consistent but less controversial. Following in President Clinton's footsteps won't be easy, but it's there for the taking.

Meanwhile back at the House, the turmoil of the Speaker selection creates opportunity for the Democrats, but the challenge should be based on more than the vote on impeachment. The distribution of the economic improvement should be discussed but not with a view toward socialism. I think the middle class should be solicited for its input as to how to improve the quality of their lives. The steadiness of the economy should allow for some high-mindedness.

Christmas Eve 1998

The impeachment process continues to tread water. The Clinton Presidency will be tainted and yet the economic accomplishments have been significant. I always succeeded in getting letters to the editor published in the New York Times when I indicated how obstinate the Republicans were about the Clinton economic policies when the results were so dramatic. Essentially Vice President Gore can run the clock until the election as long as the Fed cooperates. The domestic economy remains strong, the foreign situation appears to have stabilized and the confidence of consumers remains high. The same mantra will work in 2000 that worked in 1992, to wit, it's the economy stupid, don't forget education and improve health care. If the voter believes a candidate is trying to focus on issues that touch their everyday lives and that they can comprehend, as opposed to Trade sanctions or global environmental issues, there is a good chance the Gore Presidency will evolve from the Clinton Presidency, even if the latter limps to the finishing line. Cw: Voters want change. Ps: The Campaign that shows accomplishment will prevail.

As a sign of subtle change, voters changed party registration after the last House elections. I believe voters will vote against a candidate or his party instead of for the candidate. The lesser evil approach will be a factor. The center will be attracted by raging moderation, which was the description of Congressman Christopher Shays' position. His mantra was that the impeachable offenses haven't been proven and the proven offenses don't warrant impeachment.

The time to fix the roof is when the sun shines in. The Gore team should be doing the building block phase of the campaign to thwart serious challenges. Let the Republicans bloody themselves and follow Tom DeLay over the cliffs.

An article about Harold Ickes, the former deputy chief of staff to President Clinton, indicated why public service during a private career could be treacherous. It cost him $300,000 in legal fees. His law partner asked the question is it worth it?

It is difficult to attract talent if you don't pay too much. Many elected officials are there for the power and the stepping-stone to lucrative private sector positions. I guess a Congressman learns good people skills.

Bill Bradley seems to be the only outsider to join the race for the Presidency. Personally I find Bill Bradley a thoughtful, decent person. It is hard for any anti politician to become President. I recall Michael Dukakis as the example of a foolhardy approach to campaigning. Instead of taking advantage of the bounce from the Atlanta convention, he retreated to

Nantucket for vacation. A Presidential campaign isn't business as usual.

The New York Times called for campaign reform. It doesn't seem possible. The power of incumbency and the insatiable need for funds effectively limits reform. The Sunday pundits on ABC, specifically William Kristol, the Republican spokesperson, see Bill Bradley as a viable alternative to Al Gore. Politics is an overnight business so one never can say no to any of the possibilities particularly with someone like Bill Bradley who is persistent and a veteran politician.

Ironically, the impeachment process is putting the nail in the coffin of the Clinton Presidency, which is really on its way out anyhow. The clock will tick and the consequences of the impeachment trial will be almost moot by the time it is resolved.

I don't know what the new Congress will be able to achieve. The margin of votes for the Republican majority is narrow. The excitement of a Presidential campaign without an incumbent may be the right medicine to shake off the jaundiced attitude of the public.

The Republicans are taking a cavalier view towards the lasting impact of the dogged pursuit of President Clinton. The Democrats are being given a free pass in terms of setting the agenda ahead of the Republicans. Governors are starting to distance themselves from the Washington leadership of the Republican Party. As long as the Democrats keep their finger on the pulse the campaign can be a positive one on issues and an attack on the self-righteousness of the Tom DeLay brand of politics. He was in the pest control business and some of the strategy has been carried into to his political repertoire.

Fundraising

The winter lull masks the behind the scenes jockeying for money and political support. The true insiders are used to the cycle of the Presidential Campaign, not unlike the timetable of events that precedes the professional cycle for accountants at tax time or draft choices for professional sports teams. I am not part of that crowd primarily because the price of admission is much too high for me. The fundraising is mandatory. It reminds me of a startup company that needs venture capital in order to do business and then move up the financing chain to investment bankers, and then go public and raise capital in the public markets.

Cw: Early money gets a good Senator and good government, later money gets good government. Ps: Fundraising is always the harsh reality of politics.

The political angels start early and in earnest. Lewis M. Eisenberg is the chairperson of the Republican Leadership Council. They are the centrist wing of the ever-right leaning Republican

Party, particularly in Washington. He was on the trip to Israel with Governor George W. Bush Jr. of Texas. Ironically, Jewish fund-raisers play an active role in this phase of the national election. Lewis is a good barometer of the Republican Party's prospects. The more influence he has, the better chance they have at the White House.

John McCain formed an exploratory committee and needs to raise $20 million. The staff is comprised of former Gramm staffers, which is an uncomfortable omen. He has a strong background as a POW during the Vietnam War. He is also independent on some issues, but an anti abortion position will polarize the Women's movement. The talk of the soccer mom as an influential voting bloc will be tested in the presidential race. The entire center has moved right, but the Democratic position is not as liberal. That helps in a national race and President Clinton deserves credit for shifting the traditional Democratic platform to make it more palatable to the voters.

The New York Times mentioned Senator Bradley on the editorial page. He clearly has an understated appeal and the down to earth quality may be appealing after the celebrity influence in the Clinton years. On the other hand a little glamour doesn't hurt. It is also important to showcase the stars because their wealth is necessary to raising the bucks.

I finally understand the dynamics of the horse race handicapper. The horses are not even in the starting gate but there are some names emerging. Paul Wellstone could be the Jesse The Body Ventura of the Presidential race. He is the anti image in terms of personal appearance. He's relatively short, balding, kind of like the George character in Seinfeld. He has compassion and is progressive, but it is unlikely he will get too far. Fortunately his voice will be heard and that could help broaden the appeal of the Democratic Party. John Kerry of Massachusetts is appealing. He's tall, patrician, and very accessible. He also has a deep war chest after marrying John Heinz's widow. It is difficult to see him as an alternative to Al Gore. I believe anyone of the candidates could emerge as a vice presidential candidate.

The Republicans seem to be in disarray and their brand of politics leaves little wiggle room for one ego to emerge above the competitor. There is a vacuum that doesn't have a Ronald Reagan to fill it. The group emerging in some ways is homogeneous. Is Trent Lott that different from Phil Gramm or John Ashcroft? They are in sync regarding the conservative agenda and personality wise they exude varying degrees of piety and sanctimony. In other words, the pack will remain on the right and be marginalized by the Democrats as the Darth Vaders of politics.

William Safire's column added the names of Steve Forbes, Lamar Alexander, and Jon Aschcroft to the list of Bush and McCain. I guess the retreads have a way of resurfacing. It is comforting to know that the Democrats hold the White House. It would be frightful if the Republicans were the majority in House and the Senate and had a Republican in the White House. If my predictions are accurate, the Republicans will hold a slim majority in the Senate. The election of Jesse the Body Ventura as Governor proves there is a voice of dissatisfaction in the electorate. Perot tried it nationally and it didn't work. I believe 2 parties are the limit, but the thinkers and policy makers must keep their finger on the pulse. There could be more surprises if the fund-raisers become the only means of input to the candidates. It is natural to have this filter when the cost of entry is so steep. Until someone figures out a better way, the wealthy contributors will have a loud voice in policy and the electorate will be placated. There must be a better pipeline for ideas, I guess that's how Think Tanks get financed.

I had a letter to the editor published in the New York Times. It posed the question why would anyone want to become a Washington insider? Harold Ickes granted an interview to the Times about his travails in DC. Essentially the thought has to occur to anyone that public service is of questionable benefit. The chance to do something beneficial is remote and the frustrations are enormous. But people keep flying close to the sun.

Senator Robert Smith announces his candidacy. As the Senator from New Hampshire he is assured favorite son status. It's like a trial balloon that's guaranteed to burst. The talk of the purist police on the DC morning talk show circuit indicates that we are becoming divided on social issues. Perhaps the economic success gives people the opportunity to focus on the issues since their bellies are full.

Elisabeth Dole resigned from the Red Cross and is contemplating a run for the Presidency. If you didn't like the husband you can get the wife. The debate about the impeachment exacerbates the partisan sniping. Former Senator Dale Bumpers commented on the Op-Ed page of the New York Times that the Senate discusses each issue on partisan lines. Every issue is treated as a political issue with each party taking sides, as opposed to solving the issue in a bipartisan manner. In some ways the election will be clearer with platforms on issues being clearly laid out. The voters will know where they stand since the party pundits have analyzed each issue.

After a thorough review of the current journals, it is interesting to see the subtle filtering process. As they always said, in politics, early money gets you a good Senator and good government, later money, gets you good government. The same maxim applies to presidential politics.

The pack is thinning out before the race starts. Sen. John Ashcroft of Missouri, who spent a year laying the groundwork for a White House bid backed by social conservative leaders, announced today that he will not seek the presidency but will focus on his Senate duties instead. Facing a tough re-elect contest in 2000, Ashcroft said he determined a presidential race would "substantially impair my ability" to serve well in the Senate. He was vulnerable in his Senate race which doesn't enhance Presidential prospects.

Senator Ashcroft's withdrawal may be a sign that the Religious right might remain more influential by working at the fringes and remaining out of the limelight. It also might signal the realization that they are not in the middle of the political spectrum, which is where the trajectory to the White House must stem.

The deterioration of events in DC is exhibited by the request for the President to postpone the State of the Union. This is over the edge. It is an evil example of the Republican leadership to raise doubt and accusation to a de facto conviction and strip the President of the right to perform his duties. Actually if you use the word President without the word Clinton, it keeps the focus on the office rather than the personality. Of course there are few personalities that become Presidents.

The impeachment proceedings begin. The House Republican Prosecutorial Team looked like undertakers coming into the Senate Chambers. Strom Thurmond is presiding and he is the oldest person ever to serve in Congress. The generational conflict is evident. The dichotomy between stasists and dynamists is there to see in full color. The former category is people who value constants and the dynamists are people who allow for change and react. It is like the hedgehog and fox dichotomy of Isaiah Berlin.

Henry Hyde, chief undertaker, pronounced the charges forming the basis of the impeachment. The President allegedly willfully violated his oath regarding his relationship with a federal employee and corrupt efforts to influence the investigation. The impeachment charges must be proven and the proven charges must be impeachable.

Somehow the spectacle of an impeachment trial might be a wake up call for America to participate in the process of Washington and politics.

Absence makes the mind grow smarter. Thomas L. Friedman hit the mark in "While You Were Sleeping". The impeachment trial is a result of extremism from the far right. The processional of the House Republicans delivering the articles of impeachment reminded me of funeral parlor proprietors. The pre ordained nature is not unlike Mr. Friedman's idea to impeach Governor George W. Bush at the Inaugural. I am beginning to believe there might be something in the water supply in DC that makes people self-destruct. President Clinton made mistakes but the offenses do not rise to the level to justify impeachment. The Republicans remind me of the spirits in Poltergeist that have been repressed for 40 years and are now returning with a vengeance. Jealousy is the green monster that devours its beholder and the Republicans have been jealous of President Clinton's ability to take their greatest hits and get his own hit album. So now they use the process of impeachment to continue the brinkmanship they tried with government shutdowns and ending the full faith and credit of government debt. We need more than a broom. I think a chute with a quick opening floorboard might get the speedy solution needed in the circumstances. I am not advocating violence, only some act that will penetrate the minds of the Republicans that have brought naysaying to the point of destroying the strength of a representative government. I don't know when cooler heads will prevail, perhaps in the Old Senate Chamber without the glare of the media, since that is who many of the impeachment advocates have been playing to.

The talk of Hillary Rodham Clinton running for Senate in New York is an interesting commentary on political survival. She was criticized roundly at the beginning of the Clinton Administration and now she gets high ratings and is popular on the campaign circuit. The Gore candidacy also impacts the political fortunes of Andrew Cuomo. He is withdrawing from the Senate race and will play an active role in the presidential campaign. Thus, the

Clinton Gore team is still in charge and the White House is a good place to control your political fortunes from. It beats the temporary offices with dirty ashtrays and leftover take out food trays and plates.

Cw: Incumbents are in a position of strength. Ps: Incumbents are always in a position of strength.

Gore does Town meetings in Iowa. I realized they are taking a page out of Arthur Finkelstein's guide to politics. He is an advisor to Republican candidates. His theories say that you should ignore the opponent, set the agenda and stay on the attack. Gore is clever to echo the attitude of the President to pay attention to business as usual and not let the proceedings immobilize the White House. It is similar to the experience with normal litigation when you are expected to keep up with the case demands and not neglect the rest of your responsibilities. It is a delicate balancing act. Instead of the approach of plan your work and work your plan, it is more like being ready for anything. Not the easiest way to face the day, but I remember a White House staffer from the Bush years, Jon Podhoretz, who described the work atmosphere in the White House as hamsters on speed. The Democrats can benefit from the isolation of a Senate impeachment trial. It will create a perception from the voters that their representatives are more interested in playing out the political battles than addressing their everyday needs and interests. The impeachment trial will be a distraction and it will damage the attitude toward what it is that Washington accomplishes.

Paul Wellstone dropped out of the race with the standard Senatorial reason that he could not run for the presidency and represent his state. It is unfortunate that he leaves so early, but the liberal banner doesn't require martyrdom. If you can't raise the funds, you can't make the quest. It is like climbing a major peak without the necessary supplies. You won't get near the summit and you'll die trying.

The Administration is practicing business as usual and it will work. Vice President Gore has walked the tightrope of remaining loyal without being brought down by the follies of the President. Those follies weren't impeachable offenses and the perjury charges were flimsy. The President did not intend to mislead and the matter he testified about wasn't material. Nevertheless the political skewering continues and ultimately will become moot as the President's term ends. Vice President Gore either becomes President sooner than he thought or he gets the nomination and benefits from the backlash of the voters who were turned off by the overzealousness of the Republicans.

Cw: Voters like a slugfest with a vicarious thrill of a football game. Ps: The voters want their elected officials to provide public service.

Gore has mastered the art of continuing press. It is probably better to get consistent inside the newspaper pages as opposed to sensational headlines. The public's perception is created by the headlines but it can be solidified by the page 20 coverage about policy or summits or similar day-to-day events. The cost of fundraising comes out to $2837 per hour, which is very demanding. So how many politicians can do this?

Bill Bradley comes closer to formally announcing for the Presidency. I checked in to my Gore contact and there doesn't appear to be any formal office setup in New York. I think the race for runner up for President becomes the vice-presidential race. Accordingly, Bradley is the front-runner with fewer competitors. John Kerry of Massachusetts is personally appealing, but I'm not sure he has the capability to mount a national race.

Elizabeth Dole invites speculation about a female President but I doubt that the Republicans are prepared for that. She could make a good running mate with Bush, but I don't see that merger attitude from the Bush clan. There are 2 sons serving as Governors in major electoral states and that gives them some leverage. The New York Times made a good observation that it is important for an unlikely candidate to stay in the race in case some news destroys the candidacy of the front-runner. It is an overnight business; it reminds me of being a Broadway play understudy.

William Safire's column in the New York Times summarized the reasons that Clinton loyalists are so solid in their support. There were 7 categories and number 7 was most telling. Loyalty to Clinton in this contest is intensified by anger at his pursuers. "It's fun watching you right wing, obsessed nut-job freaks twist in the wind," fulminates a New Yorker. "This is war." A more temperate Californian notes: "The phenomenal mean-spiritedness of so many of Mr. Clinton's critics elevates him by comparison. People grow weary of negaholics." The key word here is comparison. If Bill Clinton ran against himself he would lose, but he ran against Bush and then Dole. Now Gore will run against Bush and by comparison Gore will be more positive, compassionate and in tune with the electorate.

Eyewitness

I actually traveled to DC to take care of unfinished business. We attended the impeachment trial. The negaholics have their day. The morticians have their day. Undoubtedly actually seeing the prosecutors will be sobering, but I firmly believe the oath violations are being exaggerated for political purposes. In addition if they remove President Clinton against the will of 60% of the people, Vice

President Gore becomes the incumbent President. Of course that didn't help Gerald Ford very much.

Richard Gephardt is leaning towards staying in the House to help get the Democratic majority back in order to become Speaker of the House. It is a clever move making his political survival more likely and keeping a better balance in Congress with a Democratic majority in the House. The real question is whether the Republicans will isolate themselves so effectively that they lose the Senate. There are clear signs of division between Republican Governors and the Republicans in Congress. Let the division grow and let the Democrats take the higher ground and remain unified for the election. It could be a formidable campaign by emphasizing the negativity of the Republicans and talking about the issues that the voters relate to like social security, education, financial security and a strong defense. It is almost as if President Clinton can take a page out of Ronald Reagan's book and be upbeat and optimistic, and he can even take credit for the positive outlook for the economy and the stability of American Power.

We made it as far as the Senate Gallery, but the session ended as we entered. The Senators appeared to be going about their business as they left to ride on the underground train to their offices. I actually spoke with Senator Bob Kerrey about whether Hillary would run for Senate in New York and how

Rudy Guiliani may not be unbeatable in a statewide race. I wanted to express my disappointment that he dropped out of the presidential race, but there was no smooth way to express that.

I find it ironic that President Clinton was coming to New York as we were leaving. In the early days of his Administration I would have tried to figure out a way to attend the event but instead I was on my way to DC to pick up the suitcase I left behind which symbolizes my return to politics in a form that requires less DC presence. In fact I am persuaded that there is a reverse rule as to the ability to achieve your goals in politics or business. If you stay closer to home, you increase you strength. Whether it's fundraising for a candidate or trying to get a federal contract, you are probably more potent if you work in your own arena, than working from DC where you are inherently off balance. The timetable in DC is infinite and the sense of business risk is unknown to most of the government staff. A New York minute equals one month in Washington, D.C. Cw: 80% of life is showing up. Ps: You should have the ability to navigate in D.C., but don't stay too long.

The display in the Senate was a sight to behold. It was like an audition of Congressmen trying to be Senators. Get the hook as they used to say in vaudeville. Rep. Lindsay Graham used a folksy style recounting the earlier days of segregation and how the country survived the upheaval of integration so we would also survive the upheaval of removing the President. Rep. Charles Canady went on about the oath and a standard to apply that will brand the American people for time immemorial. It had a kind white people's gospel feel to it. It reminded me of the joy that black people get when they see white people trying to have soul. It's not in their blood. The white people represented in the prosecutorial team had no soul. They were threatening the country with damnation if we didn't stop this president from his erring ways.

Martin Luther King Day 1999

―――――――――▼―――――――――

Re: The Governor-President Bill Clinton By Jacob
Weisberg January 17,1999

Jacob Weisberg captured the contradiction that is
President Clinton. The reason the impeachment
didn't shake the country is that there is an unreal
quality to the theatrics. Inside the beltway tells us
that the playbook is very confined and not available
to the American people. President Clinton sensed
the schism between the Washington professionals
and the millions of citizens that vote. The board of
directors may be critical of the chairman of the
board, but the shareholders keep him in power
because the dividends are streaming in. The Clinton
Presidency made the White House more of a
business and wasn't very private about it. The break
from the past is really just a part of the continuum
towards the blending of public policy with the

business of getting elected and staying in office.
President Clinton instinctively understands the
public and their desire to be lead and entertained.
His Houdini-like rebounds are part of the ebb and
flow of events that he doesn't control but he can
react to in a manner that blends the interests of the
American citizens and still lets him practice self-
preservation. The Governor's mansion approach to
the White House makes sense. President Clinton
understands that politics doesn't change when you
leave the governor's mansion. The goals are modest
but the perception of success increases because you
lowered the expectation level. The re-calibration
took place in the early days of the Clinton Presidency
when the major initiatives failed because they
strayed from the limited social contract. Luckily the
President was nimble enough to recognize the
eroding support and shifted strategy quickly. The
Republicans are angry with the President for taking
traditional Republican issues and placing his
imprimatur on them. You may not trust him
personally but the American people trust him as
President. The ruthlessness required to make it to
the pinnacle of political power is an accepted fact
amongst the players. Average citizens believe in the
idealistic view of the White House. The concept of
Senator Pothole applies in the White House too.
Policy is fine, but funds for the cause make for
loyalty. Couching private ambition in public interest
just means you are willing to play the political game

to be able to allot the budget priorities. Follow the money and then you might understand how President Clinton defies expectations and stays one step ahead of the competition.

The State of the Union message, 1999, will be delivered tonight. It will also be a blueprint of the Gore candidacy. The perception that the Republicans are going beyond the pale in pursuing the impeachment charges will harm them in 2000. The top fund-raisers and contributors are concerned that the Republican Party doesn't stand for anything. This is also due to President Clinton's capture of the wedge issues that were traditionally used against the Democrats. The division of issues that one party is better at solving than the other is not precise.

Wonks versus Warmongers

The President gave a commanding performance showing why he is the master politician with resilience that surpasses the competition. Vice President Gore sat patiently and supportively behind the President. The benefit of incumbency is the free exposure Gore gets on national television and the enhanced perception of power. The agenda set forth by the President was hopeful and touched everyone in some way. Now the Republicans are on the defensive as to what their agenda is since they have spending so much time on investigations and impeachment.

Keeping on the trajectory that each party is on, it is difficult to see how the election will not be a shift back to the Democrats in the House and possibly the Senate. Even the Republican Senators from states that voted for Clinton have to consider their position on impeachment in light of the voter reaction. The front-loaded primaries make the outcome less mysterious since a victor will emerge early. It will create a long campaign after the primaries and the hostilities will be vented far in advance of Election Day. Negative campaigning won't end and the negaholics will be cranking out their propaganda constantly and unabashedly.

The Clinton magic came back. In a scripted nostalgia trip, President Clinton and Vice President Gore and their spouses went to Buffalo and received a rock and roll welcome. It reminded me of the night at the 92 Convention in New York when they were playing Fleetwood Mac music and I thought it would alienate Middle America. I was amazed that the spirit was acceptable and the energy carried them to the finish line. The New York Times journalist covering the trip said that Gore appeared to be on energy supplements. That is a further sign that some of the charisma and give and take from the audience to the person speaking is also reaching Gore. President Clinton feeds off that energy and I hoped it would rub off on Gore. It has. Even Pat Robertson described the State of the Union message as a home run and that the removal of the President won't happen. Now the Christian right has cover in Robertson's observation.

Cw: Gore is wooden. Ps: Clinton's techniques rubbed off on Gore.

The decision to continue the impeachment trial will come soon. The presidential sweepstakes continue as a backdrop. Governor Bush is hesitating because his wife isn't supporting the race. Dan Quayle has come out of the woodwork. In a bizarre act of God, a tornado swept through Arkansas and hit the Governor's mansion including Chelsea's tree house. I don't know what significance it has, but it is a strange event. Clinton manages to stay out of harm's way. I believe the GOP is heading south and doing it rapidly. Assuming the economy stays stable, and the obsession remains to impeach President Clinton, the Democrats will prevail provided they address issues and keep the focus on substance as opposed to wedge, social issues.

Stalled Republicans

The Republicans are desperate. The House Republican managers are flying Monica Lewinsky to DC to determine whether she would appear before the Senate. The lack of new names for the Republican nomination indicates the stalled status of the party. Newt Gingrich rode into the sunset and the spokespersons are few and scattered.

The Monika strategy, it's still working. Cloaking themselves in the Constitutional Protector Robes, the Republicans are cannibalizing themselves. Perhaps the Super Bowl will save them. It appears the need for witness questioning has become paramount to the fair trial requirement. Somehow the concept of res judicata becomes familiar. The testimony has been taken and reviewed by the Starr investigators and brought before the grand jury. Assumedly the House staff has pored over the documents and there is also the published Starr Report.

The need for public humiliation of Clinton is consuming the House Prosecution team. Meanwhile Election 2000 looms on the horizon. Being an occasional C Span consumer, you get a chance to see Steve Forbes on the circuit. Somehow there is a sense that his previous failed attempts place him in the recycle bin. We're getting another chance to consider the decision to delete him from the radar screen, but usually your first instinct is your best instinct.

Cw: Challengers have little chance of prevailing. Ps: It ain't over 'til it's over.

I realize that I am in the minority in terms of my interest level in the primaries at this stage. I tried to consider more "what if" scenarios to avoid a fait accompli approach to the campaign. For example, what if Bradley shows strength as a challenger to Gore? The expectation is that Gore is invincible so a good showing on the part of Bradley will raise questions as to the need for more time to see if Bradley can take other states. All of this will unfold rapidly because the primary season is so frontloaded. The same is true for the Republicans. What if Governor Bush makes a mediocre showing or Lamar Alexander starts appealing to the centrist Republicans? Food for thought considering the policy and agenda voids coming from the Republican right in Washington.

The Republicans are attacking a non-candidate, George W. Bush. It seems like a remake of the resentment that many Republicans had against President Bush and his having a silver spoon in his mouth. Imagine how they feel towards his son?

Former Sen. Bill Bradley opened his campaign for the Democratic presidential nomination Monday, saying his life story and political philosophy make him a better candidate than front-runner Al Gore.

"I had a life before I got into politics and a life after I left the Senate," said the Hall of Fame basketball player who resigned from the Congress in 1996.

Bradley declared, "I am not really running against Al Gore," but the former New Jersey lawmaker repeatedly drew subtle distinctions between himself and the vice president, the son of a Tennessee senator who entered politics at a young age and rarely wandered far from Washington.

"I have not been a part of the partisanship that has shaped the debate the last couple years," he said, trying to position himself as an anti-Washington Democrat despite his 18 years in the Senate.

Upon reflection I realized that Bradley would bill himself, excuse the pun, as the "Un Gore", similar to the uncola that was used by Seven Up. It is precarious to run for office based on what you're not. It is ultimately more inspirational to your supporters to be for a position and set of values than against the front-runner.

Cw: Challengers are underdogs. Ps: Underdogs are intriguing to voters for a limited time.

I feel stronger about the prospects for the Democrats after speaking with a fellow I know locally who always is awkward despite his wealth and penchant for pro environmental issues and managing a foundation. He is an example of the lucky sperm club, as in it was a good thing his father started the business and he could maintain it. Be that as it may, he said he was hedging his bets and going to a Bradley fundraising event. The real good news is that he is considering Pataki as a presidential candidate. Then I knew the outlook was positive for Gore. Pataki is another conservative who makes the right noises on the environment and then people think he is moderate. I don't see it that way. To me he is an empty suit who D'Amato manipulated into the governorship. Pataki was in the right place at the right time, but I think he should stay in Albany. He was a member of the Legislature and now that he is in the Executive chambers, he's reached his peak.

The split Presidency continues. President Clinton attended Senator Lawton Chiles' memorial service while the Senators review the witness issues in the impeachment trial. The Vice President gets good visibility at the State of the Union and at the Pope's visit to St. Louis. The entire apparatus is in place to elect Gore and was actually moved into place as early as the Clinton re-election. I don't see how a populist challenge that is under funded has any chance. Republicans are dispersed and the visibility of some Senators during the impeachment trial might whet some presidential appetites. Every Senator believes he or she would make a great President.

Vice President Gore is so ingrained in the media tableau that he wasn't identified as he stood with the Pope and the Governor of Missouri and his wife. Once you're an icon I have to believe it makes electability more likely. The press gave some coverage to Governor Bush who is playing the undecided game in order to stimulate suspense and interest in the campaign. I find it hard to believe the decision hasn't been made. I mean how often do we wake up and say I think I'll run for President today? The political rituals approach the absurd at times. It reminds of the ritual where the nominee doesn't attend the convention until a certain point. I remember leaving the '92 convention in New York and finding out that the hubbub I noticed in my route home was Clinton breaking tradition and entering the convention arena with Hillary and Chelsea. I thought it was great idea. After all, you were getting free airtime.

The partisanship of impeachment is much lamented, but what would you expect, abstract constitutional niceties? The Senators play hardball but cloak it in gentility. It's all in the game as the song used to say. All in the wonderful game called political warfare.

The announcement of the 5.6% growth rate says a great deal about Gore's prospects. Don't change horses in midstream as they said in Wag the Dog, a movie about the election campaign of a President on the defensive about sexual indiscretions. It's still the economy stupid and smart.

New Hampshire is opening the hunting season. Dole and McCain are coming besides Forbes and Alexander, and Bradley announced there last week, with Gore scheduled for this week. The New York Times reported that it was the presence of the media that made the events official and started the season.

Conservative activist Gary Bauer, saying he has a vision for the country that will excite the American people, announced Sunday his intention to run for the Republican nomination for president.

Bauer, 52, admitted, "A lot of Americans probably don't know me yet" but said he has the conservative credentials and money-raising skills necessary for a viable candidacy.

The Republicans as moralists. There is a preoccupation by the Republicans to moralize. Fortunately the citizenry resist party platforms that seek to dictate social values and morals. That doesn't mean there can't be sensitivity to certain social issues, but not to the exclusion of economic issues.

Cw: Americans need morality. Ps: Voters resent others telling them what's moral.

The pre announcement press attention game is being artfully performed by John Kasich, Dan Quayle, and most of the other candidates. It makes sense to get as much free press as possible. The humor of the coming lineup was typified by the biography distributed at the economic conference in Davos, Switzerland. The description of Vice President Gore included Dan Quayle's information. Perhaps the better omen is that Governor Christy Whitman broke a leg.

Minority Leader Gephardt decided not to run which makes great sense. He has a good chance to be Speaker of the House when the Democrats take back the House in 2000 and a challenge to Vice President Gore would probably be a loser for him. As for Senator Bradley, a respected colleague of mine asked himself, if I won't support him against Gore who will? He is from New Jersey, likes Bradley, but is disappointed that he absented himself from Washington when he decided not to run for the Senate. So the choices continue to narrow and it portends an organized election for the House and the Senate behind a strong national ticket.

The impeachment trial is winding down and the damage to the Republican Party is front-page news in the New York Times. The approval rate gets lower as the trial proceeds. Meanwhile, Vice President Gore's candidacy appears imminent, while the Republicans are cannibalizing themselves. The list of non-invitees to a Sacramento, California convention is almost as long as the invitees. The conservatives have submitted questionnaires to candidates including a question about putting a nativity scene on the White House Lawn. Ever hear of the separation of church and state?

Sore Losers

The economy stays steady and the Republicans keep flailing away at the President. I think the deposition presentation is the death rattle of the persistent sore loser status of the Republicans. They are bitter that they lost the White House, and it happened twice to a man that doesn't embody the values of the religious right. So you keep pounding at an improper relationship hoping that other violations will fall from the tree. Now that the end of the impeachment trial is approaching, the need to look forward and use the anti-Clinton forces as a rallying cry is clear. Vice President Gore has the benefit of associating himself with an Administration that has governed during the longest economic recovery since the 9-year recovery that ended in 1969. So we are faced with a choice between moralists and doers. Is that a difficult choice?

The end of the impeachment trial marks the beginning of Election 2000. After all, President Clinton will be running the clock and maintaining the status quo of a stable economy and an improved perception of the Democratic Party and its ability to address the issues that are meaningful to the electorate. The next question becomes whether there are issues that arouse enough passion to get volunteers to work on the campaigns and help fund-raisers successfully raise money.

The nitty-gritty day-to-day campaign is anything but glamorous, but it's the only way to get there. The town meeting has become the model of citizen outreach. So much of campaigning is based on perception and momentum. There is always a concern to avoid peaking too early; on the other hand, the image of invincibility can be very pivotal in rallying the forces and raising money.

Cw: The winner of the sprints in the early primaries becomes the candidate. Ps: The Presidential race is a marathon.

The coy indecision of George W. Bush, known as "W" continues. I guess the media age makes indecision more interesting than a final decision to shoot for the stars. The Christian Coalition is making its impact in the early stages of the New Hampshire primary. After apologizing to Pat Robertson for his intelligent observation that the votes weren't there for impeachment and that President Clinton has won the public relations war, the conservatives still hold out the hope that their rabid resentment of the President will bear fruit.

The sentiment against the Republicans seems pervasive. After a $40 million investigation and dragging the country through the mud, the President will remain in office. The right wing of the House Republicans is so hell bent on destroying the President that they missed the fact that they have destroyed themselves. Jealousy is the green monster that devours its beholder. Shakespeare got that one right.

The Democrats still have their work cut out for them. There are people who aren't enthused about Vice President Gore, but that may prove to be his strength. There will be a desire for the steady at the wheel approach and Gore exudes that quality. He also has the ability to laugh at himself and that is a vital quality. Part of the Republicans' problem is that they take themselves too seriously.

Elisabeth Dole said all the right things and seemed to use the same invocation to rally the troops, let's bring back Reagan conservatism. History moves so swiftly that the memories of the Reagan Presidency as shining example of the goals we should now seek is rolled out to stimulate the troops. I think Elisabeth Dole is really Bob Dole in drag, just more rehearsed and packaged.

The invincibility of Vice President Gore continues to characterize the press reactions. Come to think of it, it isn't so surprising considering the high approval ratings of President Clinton even while the Senators are casting their votes for his removal. Gore is inextricably connected to this White House, which will prove to be an asset in 2000.

The beat goes on. As President Clinton contemplates the end of impeachment, talk of revenge against the House prosecutors by the

President draws attention. Why this is a surprise to anyone is unclear. The power of the President and an attractive Vice President as his heir is formidable.

The cat and mouse game of Governor Bush will end soon and assumedly the Republicans will have their candidate early. It will still be the economy, and education and no one can forget health care. Now you can add Social Security and the lack of financial security and the issues will crystallize.

As the final vote on impeachment is taken, it is satisfying that the sensible minds prevailed. There were few surprises, but it frees up the President to really focus on the job. Gore's stature will be maintained and the Republicans will be brutalized by their conservative members. The fate of the Presidency is determined by a hand full of people. The light is brighter for the Democrats because this experience has been a catalyst and will bring out activists.

The return to the agenda is paramount. The President will truly get back to work and Gore can become the transitional President. The sight of Phil Gramm with his maddening drawl reminds us of the core of the Republicans, principled to a fault.

Valentine's Day and President's Day. Two antithetical concepts. The question is, is politics a gutter practice, or does it reflect the methods practiced in the private sector which is played out more publicly in the political arena?

Cw: Politics is the second oldest profession after prostitution. Ps: The method aren't that different. You're always selling yourself.

Congressman John Kasich of Ohio announces his candidacy for President. It was evangelical in nature, and there were some populist buzz phrases that were subtle but a source of concern. Every Republican seems to invoke the Reagan years in a way that sounds as if he's already dead. Kasich also thought Billy Graham's oratory should be followed. He also criticized the media elite, the higher learning elite, and the Hollywood elite. Elite attacks have always been thinly veiled threats to minorities or intellectuals and have frequently led to division or hatred.

The Learning Channel had an engaging documentary about the Clintons' power marriage. Their arrival in Washington was disruptive to the Washington "cave dwellers", the people that are always in DC regardless of who is President. I was gratified by the description "cave dwellers" because it indicates the regressive approach taken by the senior career officials to new ideas. Vice President Gore actually has more experience with the cave dwellers and it will help when he is elected.

Letter to the White House
William J. Clinton, President of the United States
1600 Pennsylvania Avenue NW
Washington, D.C. 20500

Re: The Legacy of Hyde Park, N.Y.

Dear President Clinton,

I will always remember that cold day when you spoke at the Middle School in Hyde Park, N.Y. and I had an opportunity to speak with you about the economic plan you were proposing. It was a thrilling moment and it is hard to believe it has been 6 years since that visit.

Now that there is serious speculation about the First Lady becoming a candidate for Senate from New York, I couldn't help but think of the legacy of the Roosevelt's. You are prohibited from running for President because of the two-term limit following the Roosevelt years. Nevertheless, the First Lady has been compared to Eleanor Roosevelt and the role she adopted during the Roosevelt Presidency. So it is historically ironic that the promise and talent of the Clinton's can remain in public consciousness if the First Lady succeeds in winning the Senate seat in New York.

I wanted to weigh in and say that it would be a natural extension of all of the groundwork you laid during your Presidency, to say nothing of your accomplishments, if Senator Hillary Rodham Clinton becomes a reality. You have symbolized progressive ideas since the day you took office in 1993, and that tradition can continue. I hope the decision to support Hillary for Senate will evolve naturally, but I can't help but think that it is part of the Roosevelt legacy that encourages all of us to take the next step in our careers that pushes the envelope even further than we ever anticipated. I remain.

Sincerely, Steven A. Ludsin

Cc. First Lady Hillary Rodham Clinton
    Vice President Albert A. Gore Jr.
    Erskine B. Bowles, former Chief of Staff

The impeachment gave extra impetus to Gore's candidacy. He was dispatched to stand in for the President and it enhanced his stature. Meanwhile the new speaker is under pressure to produce. The intense focus on the impeachment stalled the legislative agenda, but common wisdom is that nothing much happens in the beginning of the new Congress. The possibility of Hillary's candidacy for Senate in New York gives continued life to the Clinton legacy. It will also give more attention to the New York voter and tap the funds. Schumer's victory restored the Democratic Party on the state level and this will help Gore and Hillary if she decides to run.

Senator Robert Smith of New Hampshire throws his hat in the ring for the Republican nomination and the party isn't pleased. He will dilute the results of the New Hampshire primary since an incumbent Senator should win. He is part of the veering into the wall Republican Right. He is anti abortion and has a strong defense position. The post impeachment process creates a vacuum, but it is fraught with surprise as to who will fill it.

Monica for Congress

To the Editor,

I was entertained by Clyde Haberman's piece "If Senate Race Fizzles, Here's Monica", February 19, 1999. I believe the possibility of First Lady Hillary Rodham Clinton becoming a Senate candidate for New York is real. Nevertheless, Monica S. Lewinsky for Congress raises serious issues even if the concept was in jest. The job of Congresswoman is demanding and respectfully a fresh face wouldn't be so bad, but some depth might still be required. The idea that name recognition gets you half way there is a commentary on our faith in celebrity as leadership. When you combine that with the recognition that any Federal election requires millions of dollars just to get nominated, even a formidable candidate like

Senator Lautenberg decided it was no longer appealing to enter the fray. The poise of Monica is a plus, and New York is a peculiar market where underdogs and second chances are the stuff that energizes all of us to make it there and make it anywhere, as Sinatra used to croon. Nevertheless the desire to enter Congress to meet your career goals is understandable but the sad part is that if elected you avoid newspaper and television coverage. There lies the rub. We have entered a dangerous phase in political life when celebrity gets you to the starting gate, excessive funding gets you in the race and you could make it to the finishing line regardless of substance. I hope our democracy has evolved to a higher plain but there is cause for reflection. Monica may have unknowingly made us all think about what politics and government is all about. I guess she deserves as good a chance as anyone else.

The possibility of a Senate race between Hillary Rodham Clinton and Rudy Guiliani looms large. The differences between them are not as vast as the differences between Gore and his rival. The Republican moderates are not effective in the Republican Party. The center is much further to the right in the eyes of the Republican activists. The Democratic Leadership Council was more influential in the Democratic Party because the liberal faction was more flexible. That isn't the case with the Republican right.

Governor Pete Wilson decides against running, but I don't think anyone was hanging on to that decision. The conservatives are giving up on the moral fiber of America and the liberals don't seem very vocal. The Republicans deserve the credit for moving the agenda to the right and therefore the center is more traditional. I think Gore can benefit from staying in the middle and continuing the Clinton's third way. Bradley continues his quest and he could be a default candidate or have a better showing in New Hampshire than expected. The closeness of the next major primaries in New York and California makes a lasting challenge very unlikely.

Governor George Bush rounded up a substantial number of Governors supporting his presidential bid at the National Governors Conference in DC. The RNC chairman warned the candidates not to attack each other. The President asserted his position and in the end it seems a good time was had by all.

The dodos of New England as in the moderate Republicans in the Northeast states may become extinct but they are the ironic hope of the national party. In all probability the right wing of the party would rather go down in flames than realize extremism doesn't elect a national candidate.

Cw: The more things change the more they stay the same.

Ps: The economy has changed so drastically that things are not the same for the political landscape.

There seems to be a lull in the handicapping of the horses in the race. Life is politics, politics is an overnight business, ergo, life is an overnight business. The leader of the pack today could be the straggler of tomorrow. Assuming economic stability until the nominations, there shouldn't be too many surprises from the Democrats. Pat Buchanan's possible entry into the primary promises right wing rhetoric that will continue to depict the Republicans as the extremists and will alienate the voters.

The avalanches in Europe and a death penalty in Texas crowded out Washington and politics in the national news. Strangely you become annoyed when Washington matters permeate the airwaves and yet when its gone there is something missing. The fundraising is proceeding feverishly no doubt. I haven't done much of that since the financial strains of the contracts with the SBA. I always remind myself what the stakes are for the financial backers. If their goal is influence, then the money spent probably yields results. If the goal is an appointment, then the investment is more speculative. I always go back to the theme that it is a rich man's business.

Cw: Politics requires wealth. Ps: Politics requires more wealth than ever.

Torricelli emerges as point person for Gore with Bradley. Bush forms exploratory committee and campaign reform is revived. Kerry steps out of race. Kerry cited time and money that shows the business considerations come into play when you are seeking the top CEO of all time. Looking back on the 96 election Dole now does ads for erectile dysfunction and the president was impeached because his erectile could function. California Republicans gather and face the fact that doctrinaire battles will lead to Gore s election. Republicans in the House are the moralizing minority and Gore can defeat them without charisma. California dreaming moving the primary up didn't bring out the top dogs. Bush announces and Buchanan jumps in too. If the Republicans can be pragmatic they have a chance. Elisabeth Dole will fail with a warm and fuzzy act. Why are all the leading candidates four-letter words? Gore is behind in the polls when compared with Bush and Dole who have high name recognition without scrutiny of their positions or policies. This is good place for Gore to be at this stage America likes the underdog. Bush announces and he's called Gore lite by Republican critics.

Bush is using the empty vessel theory I won't take any positions until June 99. Meanwhile Gore starts to break out in his mini Morris theory by taking positions everyday on a series of small issues. Lamar Alexander continues to run give him credit for perseverance. There is always the possibility of default candidates like Bradley if Gore falters. Elisabeth Dole exudes too much control. George Bush evades taking positions, which shows a lack of courage. Signs of the times, I received my first fundraising letter for Gore from Tom Downey. Clinton thanks supporters and Gephardt keeps Democrats in the House. Stephanopoulos book reveals the Clinton flaws but there was also the talent. Can Gore generate inspiration? Gephardt endorses Gore on his first political road trip. The strategy of keeping the House and uniting behind Gore makes sense. Only 39 % are enthusiastic about Gore whereas Bush enjoys 50% +, but at this stage it is better to be behind and gain ground than ahead and lose ground.

Cw: You can crowd out the competition with fundraising success. Ps: You can peak too early.

3 16 99 WASHINGTON (AP)—Americans rank President Clinton No.1 among postwar U.S. presidents on foreign policy success, up from eighth place in the middle of his first term, according to a poll released today.

The survey conducted every four years by the Gallup Organization for the Chicago Council on Foreign Relations, shows support for a strong defense and for efforts to fight terrorism and prevent the spread of weapons of mass destruction.

Less support is expressed for deployment of U.S. forces abroad. And, although the poll finds that more Americans measure strength in terms of economic than military power, there is less apprehension over economic competition from Japan or Europe than in previous surveys.

As Good As It Gets

So Gore inherits high approval on foreign policy and a strong economy. As good as it gets. Gore offers a more livable world. Forbes announces as Reagan Repub. and anti abortion. Chinese spying captures the bloodlust of Republicans.

To the Editor:

I was wistful after reading John M. Broder's piece "Clinton Playing Out Presidency In Reveries and a Long Twilight". After all, if you were President Clinton, how would you feel? Furthermore is he necessarily looking back with nostalgia or is it possible that he is tirelessly maintaining his focus on the future. Although he will become yesterday's man, we still haven't finished today. Our rapid absorption of events gives us little time to savor the moment. Perhaps President Clinton has an opportunity to reflect on yesterday's glories and gain strength from them. We have become inured to the negative elements of politics in general and the specific tragedy of the personal flaws of President Clinton and the impeachment. Nevertheless President Clinton has achieved positive accomplishments in office including our strong economy and an atmosphere that permits the agenda to include improvements in education and health care. As the spotlight shifts to First Lady Hillary Rodham Clinton and Vice President Gore, the foundation for their political future flows in large part from President Clinton's political battles and successes. Life and human accomplishment are fleeting and the consequences at the top are more visible and profound. The higher the mountain the thinner the air. I think we should give President Clinton credit for his resiliency. He should be allowed to feel anger towards his excessively zealous opponents. If that helps him stay motivated, why not? We all have experienced career battles and besting your opponents is part of the game. Although Mr. Clinton plays less and less of a central role, being the most prodigious fund-raiser ever is significant. The Democrats have a chance to win back the House in 2000 and perhaps the Senate. President Clinton will leave a positive imprint on American life and 22 months in politics is a long time considering that politics, like life, is an overnight business.

Al Gore invented Internet and is down home. Pataki becomes the Bill Bradley of the Republican primary. Can humor help a candidate? Forbes advocates flat tax is he one of the flat candidates. Guiliani visits Arizona to support John McCain. Gore and Bush both are sons of famous men. Remember you don't run against yourself. Jesse Jackson decides not to run for President and help minorities on Wall Street instead. Unusual alternatives. Even if a candidate is flawed, the size of his war chest means there is minimal competition. I keep reminding myself that the advertising and media environment that we are in dictates the process. It is a variation on the smoke filled room. It's more like the cash filled chamber before you come to market. The concept of underwriting a new issue in Wall Street provides a good analogy.

Gore gets foreign policy experience via Kosovo. As I write this prediction I am reminded that I still am intrigued with politics and yet I ask the question, what's in it for me? Is it really just a rich man's game? Fundraising remains the name of the game, or if you can generate good policy ideas perhaps you can get a place at the table. Campaign strategy 2000 Richard L. Burke of the New York Times states the trick now is to deploy attack strategies without seeming to do so. Al Gore began retail politics and was well received in New Hampshire. Bradley may appeal to independent voters according to the Wall Street Journal but they don't vote in the primary. Fundraising separates the contenders and the low expectations game begins. Gore kills 2 birds with one stone campaign in NH and spokesperson on Kosovo. Gore 7mm vs. Bush 6mm.Gore is showing weakness in the polls. Gore must emerge as his own person in comparison to Clinton. Quayle running to vindicate himself, I had to remind myself he was still in the race. Bradley and McCain must raise funds while advocating campaign reform.

Gore showcases foreign policy with Primakov over Serbia. Bush and Yale frat life at Yale starts raising questions. Bush raises 7mm. Foreign policy overshadows Republicans efforts to recast image. Bush starting to get pressure to take policy positions. Bradley touts big ideas. Even the familiarity of Bush Dole will not beat the strong economy. McCain says yes but waits for Kosovo to make it official. Quayle jumps in and helps us find the moral compass. Quayle to Bush: the presidency is not to be inherited. April has been the cruelest month for Gore tying scandals of Clinton to Gore. Bradley one on one challenge to Gore has possibilities.

Letters to the Editor
The New York Times
229 West 43rd Street
New York, New York 10036
                    Re: Bradley Takes Early Party Prize

To the Editor:

I was intrigued with Richard L. Berke's analysis if the Bradley candidacy for the Democratic Presidential nomination. "Bradley Takes Early Party Prize: He Goes One-on-One With Gore", April 20, 1999. I believe Bill Bradley is ready for President and I think it is important that voters have a choice. The benefit of circumstances keeps his prospects alive and persistence counts in politics.

Although Vice President Gore occupies the enviable position of front-runner and incumbent Vice President, a challenge is not so surprising. I have been an active Democrat and have supported the Clinton Gore administration. I also respect Bill Bradley and his appeal is his understatement. I am confident that the big ideas he discusses are thoughtful.

The one-on-one dynamic generates excitement for the Democrats. The similarities of the two candidates are probably a commentary on the move to the center that President Clinton began in his first campaign in 1992. Bill Bradley is more charming than people expect when they meet him in the retail political settings of the primaries.

Nevertheless, Al Gore can be similarly engaging, so we really do have a horse race.

The notion that somehow a candidate for the Presidency had another life besides politics is quaint but outdated. The quest for the Presidency begins the first time a politician runs for office.

Bill Bradley deserves to be taken seriously and being the underdog has potential. Vice President Gore is clearly qualified to be President but he should not miscalculate the shifting sands of the political primary process. The front loaded primaries were created to rout the opposition, but if the challenger emerges stronger than expectations, the process can unravel for the front-runner. Either way, the voters will benefit by the debates over policies and the pressure to take positions on issues that impact our future.

The ultimate irony is that Gore Bradley or Bradley Gore would make a formidable team. Both men are accustomed to competition and as Bill Bradley said, "Who knows?"

Consultants

The use of consultants in Israel reminded me of the likely use of Bob Shrub by VP Gore and some role for Arthur Finkelstein or even Dick Morris by one of the Republicans. Party affiliation is relatively meaningless in the business of polling and campaign management.

Clinton's polls lower due to Kosovo which impacts Gore. Gore vs. Bradley in polls 65 to 27 and Bush enjoys higher numbers due to his name. Perception from random elderly former Texan Bush had questionable dealings with Zapata. Bradley gets Wellstone's support. Bush raises money in D.C. Bush waffles on gun legislation in Texas. Primaries are barely mentioned while the Congress votes more funds for the Serbia conflict and the Republicans bravely withheld support for President Clinton's conduct of the Kosovo crisis. Sometimes there is a mysterious void of reporting on presidential candidates. Bush is absent from New Hampshire beauty contest.

Gore could be surprised in New Hampshire or Iowa. Assumedly the quiet work of fundraising is lowering the profile of the candidates. House Republicans express support for Bush 9 months before the primary. This Bush coronation does not appear to give voters a chance to decide. Can he get away with a nomination by fiat?

Cw: The political establishment can deliver. Ps: Grassroots will prevail.

Bob Herbert of the NY Times supports the strength of Gore's candidacy, the contrarian philosophy has its pitfalls and everyone wants to be smarter than the next pundit is. Gore excels at fundraising and the NY Times Sunday magazine expresses concern it could work against him, now that's a new one. Tony Coehlo chosen as campaign chairman which is a positive. Gore has no place to go but down so he needs to take command of the campaign. Silicon Valley will have a more active role in the national election. Jesse Jackson weaves in and out of national attention with some Presidential talk but to me he is a spoiler. Rubin's retirement signals another passing of the baton from Clinton to Gore.

Bush is watched closely in the Texas legislature for the consequences of his acts nationally on hate legislation but how can you be for hate? There is some concern for getting off to a slow start expressed by President Clinton and Democrats. NY Times Sunday section ribs Gore and Bradley as indistinguishable and Gore offering micro mini ideas. Bush raises record amounts in his fortress of solitude in Texas and Gore asserts education is number one. Bradley has support in the black community and has shown courage to address the race issue. Republican Congress using weapon of ridicule against Gore which is good for Gore to have such enemies. Guns take front seat. No place to go but down for Gore.

To the Editor:
I found Richard L. Berke's analysis of Al Gore's boring qualities ironic. " In Politics, Dull Isn't Deadly", May 23, 1999, Berke quoted Richard M.

Nixon who clearly wasn't boring since he resigned after Watergate, and President Clinton, who was impeached after the Monica affair. So maybe we're ready for a different style of leadership. I have always admired President Clinton's campaign style and his magnetism. Perhaps history will show that the Clinton Administration finally recaptured the White House from the Republicans and now the voters can handle a less colorful candidate. I think Al Gore is being underestimated and at this stage of the presidential election that's probably better. America likes underdogs and come from behind candidates. So the polls may show Bush beating Gore, but that's today before the test of the national election begins. We have become enamored of celebrity but substance counts too. I think Al Gore will surprise the pundits. You don't get this far in politics to be dismissed as too bland when the stakes are this high. Al Gore is ready for prime time and President Clinton helped pave the way. Al Gore can take the positives and go forward with a fresh start. Boring is a misnomer, why don't we just think of it as the classic turtle and the hare fable.

Cw: Americans want to be seduced. Ps: Gore isn't sexy but the Presidency isn't Hollywood.

Gore and Bush are the heavies. Conservatives are splintering in Iowa. Gore gets good press for tie breaking vote in Congress. NY Governor Pataki endorses Bush. Bush stays in fortress of solitude. The nominees seem preordained.

Forbes hires advertiser to package him so once you have the product and you have the money you can sell yourself to become president. Inevitability seems to be the attitude, but of course unusual primary results could change the betting. Gore recruits women Bush climbs out of his bunker and the stealth fundraising campaign. Gore seems to be in a damned if you do and damned if you don't position. Lamar laments and Hillary runs. Hillary and NY will help Gore by energizing the voters. Gore gets endorsements from former Senators. Bush s aura of invincibility sucks oxygen out of rivals fundraising efforts. Gore probably benefits from the Kosovo settlement. Bush has his coming out party in Iowa and Gore needs to show some fight without looking defensive. Bush swamped by press looks too much like his father's son. Gore goes to Carthage, Georgia on June 16th and announces his candidacy and starts to speak his mind on 20/20 about Clinton to distance himself from the negatives of Clinton. Bradley's has a Zen campaign. The Gore kick off was energized. Lame duck status starts to set in but Clinton can still help Gore.

Cw: You don't get a second chance to make a first impression. Ps: You can always re-invent yourself.

House Republicans stayed with the NRA and watered down the gun legislation. This is good for Gore as he appeals to soccer moms. Bush continues to dazzle and keep a stride. Perhaps it is about pacing and Bush may be peaking early. The lower key candidates reflect the relative stability of our times. Bush works DC but Orin Hatch steps in. How do you put yourself in the arena unless you suspect there is vulnerability? Bradley raises the issue of trust to obliquely undermine Gore. Bush walks tightrope of insider to DC and outsider to voters.

To the Editor:

I was reminded of the reasons why I find Bill Bradley an appealing national figure when I read "The Aura Of the Aura", by Melinda Henneberger, June 27, 1999. The end of the article summarized my prediction, that the ticket will be Gore Bradley for the Democrats in 2000. Using the McGwire-Sosa home-run contest as an example, Senator Bradley wanted politics to be like that because both of them won in terms of what the competition produced for the baseball fans. Similarly, there isn't that much difference between these two candidates. They voted alike 80 percent of the time. The trust issue will be important and both candidates pass that test. So on with the primaries, but don't be surprised by the outcome. Both candidates are qualified, cerebral and even complement each other. A dignified duo would increase the chance of a Democratic victory. I should add that Bill Bradley stands out in my eyes, not because of his height, but his dignity. Years ago while I roamed the Senate hallways and I explained the merits of an idea I was shepherding through a

Federal agency, Senator Bradley asked me if I would like him to call the relevant official on my behalf. I was dumbfounded since most politicians expect you to beg them for attention and you pray they will take action. Maybe all those years of hitting the goal on the basketball courts sensitized him to the need for all of us to put one up on the boards. That is the refreshing part of his aura that he has earned by being jarringly frank.

Cw: Bradley's persona appeals to the higher minds in all of us. Ps: The process isn't academic, it's more like wrestling.

Gore doesn't excite voters says Alan Wolfe in the Op-Ed piece in the NY Times. He is a sociology professor at Boston University. "W" has no place to go but down. A visit with an aide to Gore shows lingering doubts about "W's" background. "W" raises 36.3 mm which leads McCain to accuse both parties of conspiring to stay in office by selling the country to the highest bidder. Gore beefs up team and oddsmakers call for a Gore victory. Meanwhile, Bush and Elisabeth Dole get cozy in New Hampshire. Gore becomes a grandfather. Bush waives his governor's salary. His approach would have us believe the election is this November. McCain takes on the maverick role.

Hillary campaigns in NY. Betsy McCaughey Ross commented that the carpetbagger issue is not so serious since everyone knows if you can make it there you can make it anywhere. As for Vice President Gore, he had the good omen of his first grandchild on July 4th. Gore has two feuding consultants Squier and Eskew. Preemptive politics puts unforeseen pressure on candidates. More money flows to campaigns due to prosperity. John Kasich drops out. Gore focuses on gun control.

Compassionate Conservatism

Clinton defines compassionate conservatism I like you, I do. And I would like to be for the patients' bill of rights and I'd like to be for closing the gun show loophole and I'd like not to squander the surplus and save Social Security and Medicare for the next generation. I'd like to raise the minimum wage. I'd like to do these things. But I just can't and I feel terrible about it. Clinton and Gore separation issues are coming to the fore. Bush turns down matching funds, which means he doesn't have to limit spending to $40 million. Quayle accuses Bush of buying the election.

Cw: Turning down matching funds and avoiding spending limits enhances chance of victory. Ps: Too much money and spending can alienate the voters.

JF Kennedy Jr. dies in a plane crash. There isn't any apparent political significance but it is a continuing tragedy that evokes the loss of his father and the historical shift that created. Meanwhile

Rep. Michael P. Forbes of Suffolk County Long Island is switching to the Democratic Party because the Republican Party had been captured by extremists. Bush raised more money in Texas and California then Gore collected across the country in the past three months as of July 16 99. Forbes catches Bush regarding soft dollars for courting supporters at the Iowa straw poll. Bush's Pioneers produce. Can the presidency be bought? Gore does photo-op for pro-environment in contrast to Bush. Bush proposes social services through the churches and temples. Bradley condemns soft money. Presidential campaigns overshadowed by JFK Jr. s death. It makes one question the meaning and purpose in the pursuit of the presidency. There is huge pressure to raise soft money. Democrats have a chance to show it is the party of the average person. Bush looks like he's buying the presidency. Bush's drinking discussed on Good Morning America on ABC. Gore canoes on one million gallons of water in a Connecticut river. Gore appears with Congressmen and Senators to advocate preservation of the surplus for social security and Medicare. Gore will rely on policy specific presentations such as doubling of financing for cancer research over the next five years.

Cw: Staying loose and non-committal gets you elected. Ps: Specific issues help people identify you and gain you respect for being principled and specific.

I ran into Jonathan Tisch who is supporting Al Gore. He is getting support in the Jewish community. Guess what he needed? A check.

Cw: The election is only a matter of money. Ps: Campaign workers for Bradley reached 80,000 voters in 22 counties in New Hampshire. You can't buy that. Bradley could encourage grass roots participation that could create a surprise in Iowa. Gore could appear vulnerable to the Democratic Party and the pendulum could swing. Gore came to Sag Harbor, NY and there did not appear to be much hoopla. Bush appears to have outflanked his primary opponents. Bush's early success is attributed to his late start in primary process.

Bush is tacking toward the center and sounding like Clinton according to a spokesman for the Cato Institute on the Op-Ed page of the Times. Presidential campaign wasn't front-page news. Republicans are trying to embarrass Gore about the water added to the river in Connecticut for his canoe ride.

Cw: Pettiness scores points. Ps: It will backfire and show the mean-spiritedness of the Republicans.

Bob Dole works for his wife. Elisabeth Dole was running weakly without an organization but she seeks to benefit as default candidate. Gore was making appearances before Hispanics and blacks criticizing the trickle down compassionate conservative approach. Pat Buchanan hints at leaving the Republican Party which sends a signal that

conservatives are leaving the party and the splintering of the party will help the Democrats. Gore and
Bradley were trying to get attention in Iowa while
the Republican primary became more interesting.

To the Editor:

I was reassured by Frank Rich's piece, All the
Presidents Stink, August 15, 1999. I started the
Woodward book, Shadow, in the middle and read
about the Clinton Scandal first. I found it
entertaining and really not that pious. However I
agree that the phenomenon of disconnectedness is
upon us. I don't believe Bob Woodward is a
practitioner who has distanced himself as much as
others have. The Washington Media Establishment
feeds off of the same environment and falls victim
to the blinders that inevitably evolve when all that
you see is political Washington. I have had
intermittent experience with Washington and
found that the scariest response to the question
how long are you here for is indefinitely.
Washington reminds me of the insular attitude of
the folks in the movie "Mississippi Burning", which
was: we don't want no outsiders telling us how to
take care of our problems. Accordingly, those
hermetically sealed in the Beltway will remain that
way until two things occur: the Beltway people
travel back into America, and Americans stay in
Washington for more than a day and a picture with

a Congressman. The lack of proportionality is understandable because the intake in the Beltway is highly vetted and circumscribed. If you go to the Hill, the dinners and the fundraisers, it is unlikely that balance will emerge. We are also talking about hypocrisy by the opinion makers who will overlook the human frailties of those who try to please them and skewer the others that don't make the effort. Perhaps the media's expansion has opened up the process to the outsiders and that this exposure will be the undoing of the Washington establishment. After all, if the insiders didn't anticipate the Gingrich revolution or the Democratic resurgence, maybe it is better to fade away gracefully. Fortunately a Darwinian process is at work and the Cave Dwellers will whither because Disconnect has its price: extinction. That is the strength of our Democracy, and now the message gets there faster.

Labor Day

Iowa straw poll sounds ferocious. Clinton-Gore were acting like a team again while the summer slows coverage. Bush won the straw poll in Iowa. It's the people not the pundits that determine the outcome.

Cw: Bush gets the nomination. Ps: Bush gets nomination but not by fiat.

Forbes will continue to threaten Bush due to money and Dole due to personality. Meanwhile Hatch attacks Gore and Bradley as boring. Now that's funny. Bush tough on crime. Bush began to see his drug use issue become grueling.

Gore seemed quiet while Bradley stayed in position. Bush began stumbling with questions of his past. Gore has been on the national scene, while Bush begins to feel the heat. Character matters. Gore has passed these doubts. Bush's declining Federal matching funds gives earlier payout to his competitors. The early peaking of Bush will lead to surprises. Gore and Bradley will command equal attention as the Republican field narrows. Gore trying change as a theme and Coelho takes charge. Bush seems to have survived the cocaine inquiry. Many candidates are invoking religious faith which raises problems regarding the separation of church and state. Gore is trying to represent change which can be tricky for an incumbent. Bush builds up his Texas image by acquiring a ranch.

Gore enjoys perks of incumbency. Gore has the organization and Bradley has the spirit. Senator Harkin endorses Gore.

Bradley keeps tradition of Labor Day beach meet and greet. Bradley announces the goal of wiping out child poverty and health care for all. Gore offers health care for all.

Cw: People care about children. Ps: People care about themselves.

Bush vs. Gore as of 9 9 99: 56 to 37. Gore is the underdog and the incumbent.

Cw: Polls are accurate. Ps: The underdog has appeal and Gore gets perks of incumbency and prosperity keeps Gore. Bu Christy Whitman drops out and this could be a harbinger of the weakness of moderate Republicans. Talk of Forbes for Senate in NJ began to surface. Bradley gains on Gore in NY. Bush works NY and his pal and key supporter is a liberal Democrat who owns the Chelsea Piers. Bush's business experience includes the successful ownership of a sports franchise which isn't very challenging work. A Bush adviser named Olasky espouses evangelical faith based social programs, which raises a concern with such emphasis on Jesus Christ as savior.

Pragmatism says Gore wins due to his political infrastructure. Bush unwilling to change on gun control. Bradley advocates gay rights.

Cw: Soft on guns, hard on gays. Ps: The reverse will be trend. Gore criticizes Bush on gun control. Bradley won't accept Vice Presidency with Gore. The Republicans appear more afraid of Bradley than Gore. Gore has strength in California and the Gore team is targeting California in case Bradley does too well in New Hampshire and Iowa.

Cw: Gore is vulnerable. Ps: Gore uses Bradley to spar for the main event with Bush.

Bradley calculating to go the distance past NY and California. Moynihan endorses Bradley and it may keep the momentum that Gore is vulnerable.

Cw: Endorsements from former Senators may be helpful but is there impact? Ps: Bradley is gaining in a deliberate way, and the Democratic race will be more interesting without devouring the contenders.

Bush pleads for Buchanan to stay in party. The coalition of Republicans needs the right wing to stay in power but there is a distinct possibility that the right wing will go to the Reform party and hand the election to the Democrats. So while the Republicans are arguing on the right, Clinton is convincing Democrats to stay united and support Gore.

McCain is in and Quayle bows out. Bush tries to appear invincible but McCain will be the Bradley of the Republicans. Bush saves the Alamo by attending the Ryder cup in Massachusetts instead of the California convention. Bush's arrogance leads to political gaffes.

Debates start to get the campaign into focus. Bradley and Gore are fighting for labor. While Gore changes, Bradley gets his rhythm and climbs to equal footing with Gore.

Cw: Frontrunners have no place to go but down. Ps: Bush has a steeper fall and if he gets the nomination either Gore or Bradley will beat him with substance.

Gore moved to Tennessee trying to jump-start his campaign. Bush appears like Reagan but without core principles. Bush is conservative at the core but using sensitive rhetoric to seduce Middle Americans. Gore tried to ignore Bradley and act presidential but now he must regroup.

Can Gore reinvent himself and does he have to? Bradley has appeal based on character and integrity but he also reveals possible weakness on issues. Gore shoots darts at Bradley who now acts as-front runner. Bradley is using basketball as a hook and Gore is lightening up.

Cw: You can calibrate your personality. Ps: It's human to have weaknesses. We're not electing superman.

Rejection of nuclear treaty ban and the loose Buchanan will be albatrosses for the Republicans foreign policy positions. Treaty rejection gives Clinton and the Democrats a chance to keep Republicans on the defensive with their aversion to grand ideas and talent for male bonding.

Bush goes out of his way to reach out to minorities. His extra effort tells you it's not natural. Gore was catching up in the polls and his struggle makes him stronger for the general elections. Bradley and McCain both are forces to be reckoned with. Bradley and Gore to hold 7 debates. Dole drops out and McCain becomes the most viable alternative.

The Rudy Hillary contest serves as a microcosm of the presidential race. Shrill and bitter partisan sniping-on issues designed to scare voters such as nuclear testing tax cuts and future fear. Bradley hits

Wall Street for contributions and the reasons for his success are a microcosm for his national appeal: former Senator, lecturer, former Knick, and intellectual. Bradley will respond to Gore's elbows.

McCain complains about Bush going personal. Debate between Gore and Bradley in New Hampshire, results are that no one drew blood. It's better for the Democrats if there are few differences.

Forbes can outspend Bush with projections as of are $80 million. Bush is rope a doping and Gore gets pumped while Bradley keeps his stride. Debates give some focus. Bush has remained MIA. Gore still has high-powered lobbying supporters like Downey.

Cw: Voters are offended. Ps: They realize that's how DC works.

Gore gets training to be alpha male to bolster his leadership image. Bush playing it safe with pat phrase speeches. Bush can stay ahead without risks but he's boxing himself in. Gore can be the fox to Bush's or Bradley's hedgehog. Gore is stabilizing and Bush is feeling breath of McCain on his neck. There aren't many unifying issues in this campaign.

Bush finally breaks a sweat in New Hampshire and Gore is criticized for hiring image consultant outside the Beltway. It is smart to stay outside the beltway, as much as possible, Gore grew up there and he knows that game. Bush agrees to debate earlier than January 2000. He always postpones for fear of scrutiny. Bradley keeps his stride. McCain explains his temper.

Independents will determine the New Hampshire outcome. Will the challengers last in a marathon? Is there too much Clinton fatigue for Gore to get the nomination? Image is becoming more important than substance and that is troubling. Bradley returns to sport images and Gore gets relaxed and continues to transform.

Bush starts to feel pressure of issues and reality of primary. Bradley organizes a Knicks nostalgia fundraiser in Madison Square Garden and Julius Erving says campaign is about bringing back the old days.

Gore opposes the White House decision on U.N. dues. Bradley stays strong. Any challenger had a shot at Gore. McCain feeds the contrarian views but it's hard to fight a war chest like Bush's. Bush is trying a militaristic stance. Bush is getting his foreign policy preparation from his father's former advisors. The criticism of Clinton in '92 against Bush was that he didn't have enough foreign policy experience. Bush gets a B plus for foreign affairs from the New York Times. Gore gets advice from his daughter to follow his instincts. Bradley keeps up his hard work approach and attacks Gore on fundraising. The campaign seems to be about personality traits since there aren't too many burning issues.

Gore is cutting the umbilical chord to President Clinton. Gore and Hillary are both trying to become independent of President Clinton. Bradley makes foreign policy statement timed for the World Trade Organization meeting. The Bradley statement doesn't appear dramatic except for stating we are in a new world from a foreign policy perspective and he sees it differently than he did as a Senator. Bradley's attire creates stir with his old suits and a new french blue shirt purchased by an aide. Debates among Republicans may create change in the Bush invincibility perception but it is doubtful. Gore doing better at being himself. Bush plays it safe in the first debate. Bradley and Gore facing off in an early debate. Bradley accuses Gore of distorting his health care package. McCain has a slight lead in New Hampshire.

Bush gets criticized for being an intellectual lightweight. Maybe America doesn't want the intellectual elite in the Presidency? Gore and Bradley skirmish over relatively similar positions on taxes.

Laptop and Lightweight

I have always been fascinated with politics. The presidential campaign in 2000 reminds me of the popular trend to stereotype. The laptop is Al Gore and the lightweight is George W. Bush. The other day I was in the Times Square area and I ended up on the street when Vice President Gore pulled out of the garage in the limousine. I was excited by the chance to convey the thumbs up to demonstrate my support for the Vice President. But I lost the opportunity to wave because there was Al Gore with the colorful laptop screen staring at him. It may seem trifling but compare that with President Clinton. A few years ago he was in New York traveling east in midtown and even though there were only a handful of spectators left he dutifully waved even though a few staff memos probably required his attention. Al Gore on the other hand had his face down in his sleek laptop. Not that there's anything wrong with that but why lose the moment? I recall scenes in the movie "The War Room" where candidate Clinton continued to work the crowds in New Hampshire even when the pundits thought he was finished after the Gennifer Flowers episode. Compare that to Al Gore, who seems to maintain a certain aloofness. Mind you, I support Al Gore and I believe he will prevail. Nevertheless, look at Bill Bradley's relaxed style. The laptop episode was followed the next day as I walked up Lexington Avenue. There was the entourage but you couldn't tell who was in the limo. Perhaps, there is an effort to keep non-campaign events separate from official events, but a little hand waving couldn't hurt. After all, how many Americans actually see the President or Vice President, no less meet them?

As for Governor George W. Bush, I can't help but think he's like the fellow going into his father's business. He has all the perks, but doesn't know the struggle. I also consider the fact that I am close to his generation and imagine his Yale years as charmed and not too politically inclined. The similar period at Cornell was very turbulent, but no matter where you were you couldn't avoid the issues of Vietnam and social justice and other challenges of those times. I visualize George W. Bush as the gentleman C type he admits to. It may be that America doesn't need a genius in the White House, at least in the scholarly sense. The office of the Presidency seems to require an amalgam of skills that are not professorial in nature. On the other hand the lightweight image can be devastating for W. and we all know perception is reality. I frequently purchase serious books that remain unread, so it is understandable that we don't have time to familiarize ourselves with historic issues in depth. Then again, I'm not running for President.

We live in an era of constant information and the constant need to process that input. Laptop clearly revels in the analysis, but is he a good mixer? Lightweight loves to mix it up with people but is he sufficiently thoughtful to deal with the gravity of running the country? Somehow these questions remind me of high school where everyone was categorized as jocks, nerds, hoods, etc., or the fraternity pecking order of social and smart, or just party types, or dull scholars. In the end, the voters will make the decision but the prosperity seems to direct the inquiry into personality. From my perspective, I prefer laptop to lightweight, but my father always said let people underestimate you. Maybe George W. is practicing that approach by keeping expectations low. Perhaps those new handheld electronic books will help W. and Al will just have to wait for some privacy to open up the laptop and settle for the Palm handheld device to take notes while he's on the run. Wave now, win later.

2000

Bradley has an irregular heart. Bradley defends his positions on health care, social security and education as core democratic values. McCain gains as an honest non-scripted candidate. Bradley perceived as honest by Iowa voters. Bradley almost lost his New Jersey Senate seat in 1990 because he was perceived as arrogant. The candidates invoking Christ and religion a little too often.

My first actual foray into a Gore campaign office was through former Congressman Tom Downey, a classmate of mine from Cornell. The Gore office was humble but organized. Maps on the wall, lists of people ready for action but not as much buzz as I expected, however Tipper was in town and its better to be in the field than in the office.

McCain and Bradley sign a pledge to avoid soft money. McCain bemoans the Iron triangle of money, special interests corporate lobbyists. Politics is litigation. A mix of public relations and opportunism with damaging disclosures and the public is the jury. Gore challenged Bradley to drop advertising and save the money by having debates. Bradley declined. Gore gained a few inches with the campaign ad debate choice.

McCain is a breath of fresh air with his open attitude toward the press. Bradley has been taking a page out of Reagan's playbook: optimistic with a few core issues. It sounds like Clinton's famous 14 words ala Carville, "It's the economy stupid, don't forget health care and time for change".

There seems to be an unremarkable quality to this campaign which is remarkable. Bradley must prevail in Iowa and New Hampshire otherwise Gore gets nomination. Bush lite is taking continuous drip of doubts about his depth. Bush trying to be open to counteract McCain. Republicans may regret going with their hunch with Bush.

The New Year didn't give too much prominence to the political campaigns. New Hampshire might prove to be the maverick's heaven, but does it reflect the entire electorate? Similarly victory in Iowa doesn't mean the rest of the country buys your act.

Cw: These early states matter. Ps: The later and larger states of New York and California will determine the nominees.

Differences arise between Gore and Bradley on health care, gun control and campaign reform. Gore criticizes Bradley for support in drug industry.

Letter to the Editor

I found the "Issue for McCain Is Matching Record With His Rhetoric", Stephen Labaton, January 7, 2000 thought provoking. The questions about Senator McCain's judgment are fair but I believe he has conflicting pressures created by a system that encourages constituent service and campaign contributions which are not supposed to be linked. The Senate never adopted clear standards and that leaves room for Senators to decide where the line is between service and undue influence. It is a murky area. As Robert S. Bennett indicated, tension is inevitable. The key to the riddle isn't whether campaign contributions are the reason for Senatorial action. The oversight responsibilities of the relevant Senate Committees require lawmakers to monitor federal agencies that can be arrogant and bureaucratic. I spent the last 10 years dealing with the federal agencies responsible for liquidating federal assets. The weapon of choice for federal regulators is delay or as I graphically describe it, the 3-d's: delay, defer and derail. If they don't decide, they don't make mistakes. Therefore federal regulators are comfortable in running the clock hoping that you will give up and move on to other pursuits. The effort by Senator McCain to get a decision after 2 years of agency review is a reasonable request. The hypocrisy lies in the difference between who tries to influence the process. If your opponent does it he's unethical, if you do it, it's constituent service. Either way the money pours in. I believe Senator McCain is being forthright about the "damned if you do and damned if you don't" position an elected official is in. It is extremely costly to run for office and no one expects a candidate to unilaterally disarm. The responsibilities of Senators require action and are dictated by the sphere of influence based on Committee assignments. As Chairman of the Senate Commerce Committee Senator McCain is involved with a wide cross section of business interests with a great deal of money at stake who need decisions in order to act. The goal of campaign reform is laudable and Senator McCain has exhibited courage in espousing that cause. Let's not be so unrealistic to expect him to wait for Senate action on campaign reform in order to help contributors, otherwise he would become history, not for getting legislation passed, but for getting defeated.

Elisabeth Dole endorses Bush encouraging vice presidency speculation. Bradley and Gore begin debates and they seem to neutralize each other. Campaigning is litigation.

The electorate wants unfiltered access to the candidates. Gore meetings with various ethnic groups, but can they be jumpstarted? Gore is a class act, composed, knowledgeable even presidential. Bush has loyal professionals orchestrating his quest. My nagging question about Bush is what's in the suit? Meanwhile, Bradley keeps plugging. Gore is ahead by 21 percent in Iowa according to Peter Knight, a Gore staffer. Will the establishment or the usual round of suspects be able to elect Gore? Debates are more frequent but do the voters care? Since issues are not as pressing personality means more to voters. The novelty of McCain and Bradley may be waning. McCain suggests a separate governmental reform agency but that won't happen.

Gore gets advantage with unions in Iowa. Can Bradley motivate people to go to the caucuses? Iowa is classic grass roots politics. Republicans seem to have such a crowded field it has a circus like quality. Bush is strong but politics is an overnight business and we have a long way to go, nevertheless the results are predictable because we live in prosperous times and we are at peace. An incumbent's dream come true.

Martin Luther Kings Birthday brings back the civil rights period and what impact it has today. Bradley raises the race issue often but Gore seems to have solid support. Gore's campaign manager insulted the Republicans by singling out Colin Powell and the Republican Congressman from Oklahoma, JC Watts, as their black poster children. She isn't so far off. Republicans are more reserved about bringing minorities into their tent. McCain displays a sense of humor. Bradley and Gore debate degrees of difference. Gore acting like a winner.

To the Editor,

I found "Al Gore Moves Beyond Meta", by James Bennet, January 23, 2000 insightful. The paradox of Gore's success was captured in the last paragraph, " Before Gore can hope to seem like less of a politician, he will have to become more of one." Vice President Gore revealed another contradiction of being part of the Clinton Administration when he said he knew what it felt like to follow Elvis when he spoke after candidate Clinton at the 1992 Democratic Convention in New York. I believe history has been good to Al Gore and will continue to be. We have record economic prosperity and world peace in a relative sense. The inner turmoil of Al Gore's campaign in the last few months reflected his own adaptation to being the man in front after so many years of being Vice President and behind President Clinton. Politics is an overnight business and Gore's ability to move from K Street to Nashville demonstrated a nimble mind willing to be pragmatic for the good of the campaign. It isn't easy to prepare to run for President and each candidate's personality and idiosyncrasies will dictate their fate. The notion that politics is a sordid business is a constant refrain that fails to understand the humanity of a process that is flawed because it is only human. Authenticity is a wonderful goal, but we should all understand that perception is reality and the sheer speed of the primary process doesn't leave much room for in depth analysis of the issues. Gore would dazzle most people with his command of policy but stumping for votes doesn't lend itself to opportunities to show his depth. The political operatives need to be on the ground and in the air, but the commander-candidate is on the front lines. Al Gore must curb his contempt for the business of politics and political operatives as a class. I think he has come to that realization. Although there may be a lack of passion for Gore amongst his advisers, they talk of deep respect for his decency, policy judgment and commitment to public service. That's a good endorsement in my eyes. The next election is Al Gore's to lose because of the success of this Administration's economic policies and the sensitivity to voter issues of education, health care and social security. Gore is more and he will make a style of substance in an era that could elevate public policy thanks to the economic prosperity Gore helped to create. Seize the moment.

February 25, 2000

Gore predicted winner in Iowa but Bradley will go the distance. Gore was 2 to 1 over Bradley. I guess status quo is appealing after all. Bradley goes on the attack on Gore's credibility. Bush has to watch his conservative flanks. Bradley condemns negative campaign. New Hampshire will crystallize the outcome. Mavericks may have their day. McCain's victory speech includes his iron triangle mantra: lobbyists' legislation and big money which puts special interests ahead of national interest.

March 7 is the big day for Democrats. McCain has challenge in South Carolina. Forbes drops out, which is no surprise but who does he throw support to and does it matter?

Bush's vulnerability shows money can't buy substance and he tried to declare himself a winner before he ran in a primary. Bush revives in South Carolina but there is still room for vulnerability. His mantra of compassionate conservatism and record of reform is tired and vague. Bradley stays the course while Gore is criticized for being a professional politician, which is what it takes to get elected. Running for office is like a job interview, an unpleasant but mandatory condition to getting the job. Hillary and Al pack a punch in an Albany, NY church with a message of opportunity and obligation after the longest period of economic prosperity during the Clinton Presidency.

The Gore Bradley NY Apollo Theater debate is a draw. McCain wins Michigan and Bush looks robotic. Gore is pugnacious and Bradley is perceived as weaker since New Hampshire. Gore will win in 2000.